TRUE REPENTANCE

By
Dwayne Norman

Empyrion Publishing
Winter Garden FL

True Repentance
ISBN: 978-0692230657
Copyright 2014 by Dwayne Norman

Empyrion Publishing
Winter Garden FL
info@EmpyrionPublishing.com

Unless otherwise indicated, all Scripture quotations are taken from the New King James Version of the Bible.

Printed in the United States of America. All rights reserved under international copyright laws. Contents and/or cover may not be reproduced in whole or in part in any form without the express written consent of the author.

TABLE OF CONTENTS

Chapter 1
What Does it Mean to Repent? 5

Chapter 2
True Salvation 23

Chapter 3
First Love 33

1

What does it Mean To Repent?

I've been involved in church since I was 14 years old. Over the years I've heard ministers explain why they thought many people, who claim to be saved, have continued to live in sin; but I didn't care for their answers. If you asked them why a certain "Christian" went back into sin, they would usually give about 3 different reasons. 1. No one preached repentance to him. 2. He didn't have a true conversion. 3. He got saved too quickly. Let's look at Acts 2:38 & 3:19.

"Then Peter said to them, "<u>Repent</u>, and let every one of you be baptized in the name of Jesus Christ for the remission of sins; and you shall receive the gift of the Holy Spirit."
"<u>Repent therefore and be converted</u>, that your sins may be blotted out, so that times of refreshing may come from the presence of the Lord."

True Repentance

The Apostle Peter said to repent and be converted; implying one can repent and not be converted. So just repenting doesn't automatically mean you've been converted. If it does, Peter would have just said to repent. These 2 words must have some difference in meaning, since the Spirit of God encouraged the people to do both; repent <u>and</u> be converted. According to W. E. Vine, the Greek word for "repent" is (metanoeo) meaning **to perceive afterwards**. This word is made up of 2 Greek words (<u>meta</u>, meaning after, or implying change, and <u>noeo</u>, meaning to perceive). Therefore, to repent signifies **the change of one's mind or purpose**. To repent doesn't necessarily mean the person is born again. It means the person sees things differently than he did before. Before what? Before he saw or heard some new information. After seeing or hearing this new information, he or she can now perceive things differently and change his mind or purpose. He may decide to make a change in his life, such as get saved or be converted.

As the Church, we have been commissioned to preach the Gospel to every creature. The Gospel is all of God's Word, but in a nut shell, it's the death and resurrection of Christ (I Corinthians 15:1-4). It's the message of the cross (I Corinthians 1:17,18). Also, see our book, The Awesome Power in the Message of the Cross. Based on the definition of the word

What Does It Mean To Repent?

"repent", when a lost person hears the message of the cross, and what Jesus did for him at Calvary, he will now perceive things differently. There will be a change in his thinking. He now <u>perceives things differently</u> about his life, <u>after</u> hearing the Gospel. He can now choose to believe things differently in his heart, and turn away from his old life to a new life in Christ; that's what it means to be converted.

W. E. Vine says the Greek meaning for "convert" implies **a turning from and a turning to**. When you put the two words together (repent and convert), it means that a person will perceive things differently (after hearing the Gospel message), and will turn from their old way of living to a new way of living for God.

Some time ago I was at a particular church giving an altar call, and I was quoting Romans 10:9 for any that were lost in the service. Romans 10:9, is the most informative Scripture in the Bible (that I know of) on how to be saved or born again. It says you have to confess Jesus as your Lord, and believe in your heart God raised Him from the dead. God said (not man) that if a lost person will do that, he will be saved. It just does not use the word "repent" in that particular verse. After the service, the pastor kind of nicely rebuked me for not actually using the word "repent" in my altar call. The pastor made it clear to me that I needed to tell the people to repent and believe, making it sound like I had to say that word.

True Repentance

The only problem with that is, the Bible doesn't say in any verse that every time you give an altar call you must always use the word repent. I get a kick out of the little quirks that so many ministers have in the way they like to do things. Certain things they think you have to say or do that can't be qualified with Scripture, but because they have been doing it so long, they think it's Bible. They may not be bad things, but we all need to examine why believe the way we do, and make sure we can back it up with Scripture. By telling me I did not use the word repent, shows ignorance about the very definition of the word. When I quoted Romans 10:9, I gave any lost who were there, new information, which would cause them to <u>perceive things differently</u>, so they could be converted. After learning how to be saved from the Scripture I quoted, any one there could have repented and been born again; without me actually using the word repent. Do you see that?

<u>It's very Scriptural to tell people to repent. The Apostle Peter said to repent and be converted, even the Lord Jesus said to repent and believe the Gospel</u>. But the Lord didn't say you have to always say it that way. Again, the Bible doesn't say that you must use or say the word "repent" every time you witness to someone. Don't make the word "repent" into some kind of good luck charm that evokes a special power. Always remember this: the power of God is in the

What Does It Mean To Repent?

Gospel (Romans 1:16; I Corinthians 1:17,18)! When Paul got saved on the road to Damascus, the Lord appeared to him and he said, "Lord." All we have on record was that he said, "Lord", and was born again. We know he was born again, because when Ananias came to him (Acts 9), he called him <u>Brother</u> Saul. The Bible doesn't say that Jesus said, "Paul, you need to repent and say Lord," so don't add it in there. But now watch this. Did Paul repent? Most definitely! After Jesus appeared to him he perceived things differently (that's what it means to repent), and he was converted. Remember the eunuch in Acts 8 that Philip led to the Lord? It doesn't say that Philip used the word "repent" in witnessing to him, but the man did repent. You may ask, "How do know that?" Because Philip led him to the Lord, so he must have perceived things differently.

Repentance always comes before conversion or salvation, even if you don't say the word "repent".

When people get saved after hearing the Gospel, it's because they perceived things differently and chose to turn from their old way of life to a new way of life. People can repent and turn to God whether you tell them to repent or not. In Acts 10, God sent Peter to preach the Gospel to the household of Cornelius. Verse 34 through 43 was what he preached. If you read those verses, he never said the word "repent". If you have to say that word every single time, you would think Peter would have known that. In verses 44-48, the Bible says while Peter was still speaking, before he could even give an altar call, or even pray with them, the Holy Spirit fell on those who heard the Word. They got saved, filled with the Spirit, spoke in tongues before Peter finished his sermon, then baptized in water; and you don't get filled with the Spirit or baptized in water until you're born again.

Acts 16:29-31 says:
"Then he called for a light, ran in, and fell down trembling before Paul and Silas.
And he brought them out and said, "Sirs, what must I do to be saved?
So they said, "<u>Believe on the Lord Jesus Christ, and you will be saved, you and your household.</u>"

If you read all of the story, you know that Paul and Silas were locked up in prison, but God set them free. The keeper of the prison was so affected by the miracle, he wanted to get saved. Now Paul and Silas knew how to lead people to the Lord, but if you notice in their instructions to the prison keeper, they didn't say anything about repenting. Yet, we know they repented. If you read the rest of the verses, he and his family were baptized in water. Baptism in water is a sign that you've been born again. It shows that you died with Christ, when you go under the water, and that you arose with Christ to newness of life, when you come up out of the water. In Acts 17:30, the Apostle Paul said:

"Truly, these times of ignorance God overlooked, but now commands all men everywhere to repent."

What does it mean when it says that God commands all men to repent? Well, remember the definition? God commands all men everywhere to see things differently, which implies change. He expects them to turn from their wicked ways, and give their lives in service to Him. What needs to be done for true repentance to come to people? They need to hear the Gospel. They won't perceive things differently until they know there is something different to perceive. Every time you preach the Gospel, you're preaching repentance. When you preach the good news, news from Heaven they have never heard, you're encouraging people to look at life in a new light; God's light. You're preaching to people that they need to perceive things differently, even if you don't tell them to repent. <u>They don't automatically perceive things differently just because you told them to repent</u>. You have to tell them something different to perceive, or they won't repent. We need to preach repentance everywhere we go, which is explaining to people, there's a better life for them in Christ. Repentance from dead works is one of the doctrines of the Church (Hebrews 6:1,2).

The lost need to hear the Gospel so they'll know to repent and be converted. As Christians, we need to continually hear the Gospel to maintain our salvation, and grow stronger in the Lord. I Corinthians 15:1,2 says:

"Moreover, brethren, I declare to you the gospel which I preached to you, which also you received and in which you stand.

By which also you are saved, <u>if you hold fast that word</u> which I preached to you-unless you believed in vain."

For a Believer, repentance from dead works is living everyday walking after the spirit and not after the flesh. Instead of living for the devil and yourself as you did before salvation, you now live to fully please the Lord and glorify His Name.

"For we are His workmanship, created in Christ Jesus <u>for good</u> works, which God prepared beforehand that we should walk in them."
(Ephesians 2:10)

What Does It Mean To Repent?

I think many in the Church see repentance as more of an emotional state. They assume if the person is balling, crying and blowing his nose, he must have truly repented. The truth is, he may or may not have repented. Emotions are not necessarily the test to prove if a person has repented. The test is, did their lifestyle change. As Hebrews 6 says, are they now showing us a life of repentance from dead works? There's nothing wrong with being emotional when you repent, but it's not a requirement. The requirement is, you see things differently and make a change.

I think many have the idea that the word "repent" is the same as the word "regret". In the dictionary, repent means **to feel such regret for past conduct as to change one's mind regarding it.** Regret means **to feel sorry about something**. There's nothing wrong with regret, or feeling sorry about what you did, but it doesn't mean you repented. You can still perceive things the same way, and have regret. A thief can regret robbing a bank, but not repent for it. He may cry, weep and say he's sorry, but if he doesn't perceive and understand that stealing is wrong and a sin, then he hasn't repented. He's just regretful or sorry he got caught. If he hasn't truly repented, he will rob another bank if he gets a chance. That was the condition that Esau found himself in.

True Repentance

Hebrews 12:16,17 says:

"Lest there be any fornicator or profane person like Esau, who for one morsel of food sold his birthright.

For you know that afterward, when he wanted to inherit the blessing, he was rejected, for <u>he found no place for repentance</u>, though he sought it diligently <u>with tears</u>."

This tells me that Esau was very regretful. He cried and was so sorry, but God said he found no place for repentance. That's another way of saying he gave no place of repentance in his life. He chose not to perceive things differently and make a change. The only way he saw things differently, was learning that he missed out on a great blessing, but according to Hebrews, he didn't understand enough about the sanctity of Godly things to turn from his ungodly ways to a life of Godliness. Like many Christians today, he demonstrated to us that natural things were more important to him than spiritual things. Going to a ball game (Nothing wrong with ball games. I like football.) is more important to them than going to church. Reading the newspaper has a greater priority to them than reading the Bible. The birthright was a blessing from God that would prosper Esau in every area of his life, but to him, it wasn't as important as a bowl of stew. He wasn't sorry because he understood

What Does It Mean To Repent?

that he disrespected the things of the Lord, and wanted to turn from his profane lifestyle to a life of holiness unto God. He was sorry that he didn't get something which he found out was very important. He was just mad because he lost the birthright. Again in verse 17, God said he was rejected from receiving the blessing because he found no place for repentance, which means he did not exhibit true repentance; even though he was very emotional. The Lord knew what was in his heart. Even though he didn't like losing this blessing, he still did not perceive things differently and turn to the Lord to please Him. Only God knows what's in people's hearts. Whether we are emotional or not, He sees our hearts and minds, and knows if we have found a place of repentance.

II Corinthians 7:9,10 says:

"Now I rejoice, not that you were made sorry, but that your sorrow led to repentance. For you were made sorry in a godly manner, that you might suffer loss from us in nothing.

For godly sorrow produces repentance leading to salvation, not to be regretted; but the sorrow of the world produces death."

It sounds to me like there are two kinds of sorrow. Worldly sorrow and Godly sorrow. Godly sorrow will produce repentance, but worldly sorrow produces death. Esau had worldly sorrow, didn't he? He found no place for repentance. In the Greek, the word "place" is "topos" meaning <u>condition or opportunity.</u> He found no condition in his heart to repent. He did not want to take the opportunity to repent, even though he was sorry. Therefore, his sorrow was worldly sorrow, and not Godly. Think about Judas. In Matthew 27:3-5, the Word tells us that after Judas betrayed Jesus, he was remorseful and brought the 30 pieces of silver back to the chief priests and hung himself. From his story, we know he had worldly sorrow which produced death for him. The Lord Jesus said, **"…It would have been good for that man (Judas) if he had not been born."** (Matthew 26:24) Remember what Peter said, in Acts 1:24,25, when the Apostles were considering who would replace the office of Judas.

"And they prayed and said, "You, O Lord, who know the hearts of all, show which of these two You have chosen,
To take part in this ministry and apostleship from which Judas by transgression fell, that he might go to <u>his own place.</u>"

Based on these Scriptures, it sounds to me like Judas did not make it to the Father's place, the place of a right relationship with God. Acts says he went to his <u>own</u> place, which obviously was not a place of repentance. He and Esau had worldly sorrow, but not Godly sorrow. On the other hand, you have Peter denying Jesus in Matthew 26:69-75. The Word says Peter went out and wept bitterly, so they both had sorrow. We know that Peter had Godly sorrow and repented to the Lord. You may wonder how we know that; because we know the rest of Peter's life. We know that his Godly sorrow produced repentance, which led to his salvation. Look at the results that come from Godly sorrow.

"For observe this very thing. That you sorrowed in a godly manner: What diligence it produced in you, what clearing of yourselves, what indignation, what fear, what vehement desire, what zeal, what vindication! In all things you proved yourselves to be clear in this matter. (II Corinthians 7:11)

Let me remind you that a man in the Corinthian church had committed sexual immorality. The Apostle Paul told them to send him out of the church, to deliver him to Satan for the destruction of his flesh, in hope that he would repent and his spirit would be saved (I Corinthians 5:1-5). After the man had repented and came back to the church, they were not so eager to forgive him. So Paul had to encourage them to forgive him and reaffirm their love to him (II

True Repentance

Corinthians 2:3-11). Now listen to II Corinthians 7:11 out of the Living Bible.

"Now I am glad I sent it, not because it hurt you, but because the pain turned you to God. It was a good kind of sorrow you felt, the kind of sorrow God wants his people to have, so that I need not come to you with harshness. For God sometimes uses sorrow in our lives to help us turn away from sin and seek eternal life. We should never regret his sending it. But the sorrow of the man who is not a Christian is not the sorrow of true repentance and does not prevent eternal death."

There's another word I want to look at that the world could confuse with the word "repentance". The word is "reformation". This word means **to form again and renew**. It has a good, positive definition, but it's not synonymous with being born again. It also means **to change for the better, to give up irresponsible or immoral practices, or a movement that attempts to institute improved social and political conditions without revolutionary change.** The problem is, it's all about works (human effort apart from grace), man trying to correct his lifestyle by his strength and ability; not realizing that his real problem is a spiritual problem. It's very

What Does It Mean To Repent?

commendable and honorable that he wants to put forth an effort to be a "better" person; that's why he makes New Year's resolutions. He decides he's going to be more loving and kind to others, feed the poor and maybe go to church a little more. Of course, I would rather him do that, than to decide to act more ungodly. But, the only way for man to truly change his outward lifestyle, and ultimately change society for the good, is to experience a radical change inside. He must be changed from the inside out! He must receive a new nature! And he <u>can't</u> give himself a new nature! Therefore, he must be born again through faith in Jesus' shed Blood! And that will never happen through reformation, or trying to reform one self. That kind of drastic change, which is becoming a brand new person in Christ, only comes through repentance and conversion!!

Reformation is good, but it's not the best. The Apostle Peter didn't say reform and be converted. He said repent and be converted. Reformation deals with wrong <u>doing</u>. Sin is mainly wrong <u>being</u>. I want you to really think about that. Think about the difference. The reason man does wrong or sinful things, is because his being or nature is wrong. He needs a new nature. The Old Testament laws couldn't give man a new nature (or cleanse his conscience). Man could only be ceremoniously cleansed or cleansed on the outside through the shedding of the blood of animals,

True Repentance

that's why the Lord Jesus had to come and fully represent us. The Lord Jesus came to destroy man's sinful nature (in his spirit), and make him into brand a new being. He gave him a new nature in his spirit, and cleansed his conscience (II Corinthians 5:17; Hebrews 9 &10). Even repenting, seeing things differently and wanting to make a change, won't give a person a new heart; only Jesus can do that. You must receive Jesus as your Lord and Savior to be born again and to enter the Kingdom of God (Romans 10:9). First, you must recognize you need a Savior; that's what repentance is about. When Christians repent, they're not getting saved again, but they're perceiving things differently about their lives. They're recognizing sin in their lives, and choosing to turn away from it back to God. In Matthew 3:8, John the Baptist said: **"Therefore bear fruits worthy of repentance."**

Have you ever heard this comment before? "He doesn't look like he's repented." Many times Christians consider a bold emotional display as evidence that a lost person has repented and been born again. They don't think the person got saved if he doesn't show an emotional response. The problem with that is, they're only looking at the physical house (body) that the real man (his spirit) is living in to make their judgment call. Man's heart or spirit is what gets changed, and God is the only one who can see that. So, we need to be very cautious about judging someone based on an emotional response. The Bible does say that if a person has truly repented, at some point he will bring forth fruits of a changed life. I don't have to study the chemical makeup of an apple tree to know it's an apple tree. If an apple tree could speak, it wouldn't have to convince people it's an apple tree. Its fruit would be all the evidence required. In Acts 26:19,20, Paul said:

"Therefore, King Agrippa, I was not disobedient to the heavenly vision,
But declared first to those in Damascus and in Jerusalem, and throughout all the region of Judea, and then to the Gentiles, that they should repent, turn to God, and <u>do works befitting repentance</u>."

We shouldn't have to try to convince people we're Christians. That should be evidenced by our fruit. What kind of fruit? The fruit of speaking and obeying God's Word, and walking in love and holiness. We should show forth works befitting repentance, or you could say it this way; the works in our lives should prove that we are seeing things the way God sees them (from His Word), and making the correct changes or adjustments in our daily lifestyles.

True Repentance

2

True Salvation

There's a very destructive false doctrine working its way through the Church world today concerning when a person is genuinely born again, or when does he get saved. This doctrine states that every human being is already born again or saved, whether they accept Jesus as their savior or not; because of the fact that Jesus died for the entire human race. These people who claim to be Christians don't believe that you must repent and be converted, as the Apostle Peter said. I was talking to one "pastor" who told me to my face that when Jesus said to go make disciples of all nations (Matthew 28:18-20), He wasn't saying to get them saved first. This man said everyone is already saved, or that salvation automatically happened for all people when Jesus died and arose from the dead. He said they just need to be discipled now. The only problem with what he said to me was, it is totally un-Scriptural, and Biblically wrong! It's hard to believe that a person could read the Bible (I'm

True Repentance

assuming he does) and still be that spiritually blinded.

When the Lord told the Church to go make disciples, He was telling us the end result. He knew they must be birthed into the Kingdom before they could grow into spiritual adults. If I told a couple who just got married, to go and make adults, they should know what I meant by that. They should know I'm telling them the end results produced from having children. They should know that I meant for them to make babies first, but don't stop there. After they're birthed into the world, then disciple and raise them up to be mature adults. Disciples come from converts to the Lord, and converts come from non-saved people who have heard the Gospel, repented and have come to Jesus to experience eternal life, which He provided for them through His death and resurrection.

One great minister of the past century said there is a legal and vital side to our redemption. Meaning, everything God did for humanity in Christ at Calvary is already legally done. Hebrews 9:12 says that Jesus obtained (past tense) eternal redemption for us. He finished everything for us about 2000 years ago. Legally speaking, He obtained salvation, healing, protection, prosperity, joy, peace and righteousness for the entire human race, but the Bible doesn't teach that those wonderful blessings will automatically appear in our lives. The Word talks about grace and faith. Grace tell us that all those redemptive benefits are freely ours right now (legally), we cannot earn or merit them. But, even though Jesus has already obtained them for us, we still must receive them.

What if someone opened up a bank account in my name, and deposited $100,000 in it? If they said there were no strings attached and it's freely mine, would it automatically appear in my hands at my house? No. I would still have to go get or receive it from the bank. I would not be earning it by going to the bank and making a withdrawal, because it's already been given to me. Why would I need to earn something that's already mine? Even though the financial gift is free to me, I would still have to believe (faith) and act on the word of the person who blessed me, and make an effort to appropriate what's already mine. Even though the money is mine, it could not withdraw itself from the bank for me.

This particular "pastor" doesn't understand the difference between works of faith and works of the flesh. He actually told me, if you have to operate by faith, then it wouldn't be by grace. If you know the Word at all, you know his statement is the opposite of what God says. Romans 4:16 says:

"Therefore <u>it is of faith that it might be according to grace</u>, so that the promise might be sure to all the seed, not only to those who are of the law but also to those who are of the faith of

Abraham, who is the father of us all."

God (who cannot lie) said it has to be of faith so it can be of grace. Meaning, the only way you're going to receive freely from His grace, is by faith, and if it is of faith, we can only receive by grace. That verse means you can't receive anything by grace, if you don't operate in faith. God's grace only works for us by faith, or it wouldn't be grace. Again, operating in faith can't be trying to earn something from the Lord, or it wouldn't be by grace. Everything we have in Christ has been given to us from God's grace. It's all free, but we must operate in faith to experience these things. It seems that many Christians mistake works of the flesh, for works of faith. I think they get confused, because they don't understand the difference between works of the flesh in the book of Romans, and works of faith in the book of James. In Romans, Paul said you're not justified by your works; only by faith in God. In James, the writer said faith without works is dead or useless. You have to study both of these books and you'll see they are talking about two different types of works.

The Apostle Paul was trying to persuade the Jews, in the book of Romans, that no matter how successful you are in obeying the law, it won't cleanse your conscience or give you eternal life. He was teaching them that only faith in Jesus will give them a new nature inside. He doesn't tell them they already have a new nature. He doesn't tell them they've been saved since Jesus died, and they just didn't know it. Listen to how Paul shows faith and grace working together.

"Therefore, having been <u>justified by faith</u>, we have peace with God through our Lord Jesus Christ,
Through whom also we have <u>access by faith into this grace</u> in which we stand, and rejoice in hope of the glory of God." (Romans 5:1,2)

To be justified means to be made righteous or born again. He didn't say we've been justified without faith, but it's by our faith. Also, he said the only way we have access into this grace is by (not without) our faith. In Hebrews 11:6, we're told it is <u>impossible</u> to please God without faith. Faith is trust in God. It's believing God's Word is true and obeying it. Romans 3:4, tells us to let God be true, and every man a liar. In other words, if your denomination teaches a doctrine that doesn't agree with God's Word, you need to quit believing it. Let's check out everything we believe with what the Bible says. Don't be afraid to question what ministers and denominations teach. Be bold to examine everything in the light of Scripture! Let's not allow pride to hinder us from receiving

Truth! In Galatians 2:16, the Spirit of God wrote this through the Apostle Paul:

"Knowing that a man is not justified by the works of the law but by faith in Jesus Christ, even we have believed in Christ Jesus, that we might be justified by faith in Christ and not by the works of the law; for by the works of the law no flesh shall be justified."

If you look closely at that verse, He said we have to believe (which is present tense) in Jesus right now to be justified, which means to be made righteous or born again. He didn't say we were already justified legally and experientially when Jesus went to the cross. If we were, then we would not need to believe in Him now to be saved or justified. There are over 100 "in Christ, in the Lord, and in Him" verses in the epistles. If you'll really read and study your Bible, you'll see God teaches us 2 sides of our redemption in Christ. First, we learn of what God finished for us at Calvary by His grace. Second, we learn that we will never experience all He finished for us without faith; we must receive or appropriate what's already been done. That will never change, no matter what your grandma or denomination teaches!

James teaches us that to operate in faith requires some type of corresponding action. If you believe the

Lord wants you to feed the poor, then you need to do that. Faith is simply obeying what the Lord tells you to do. If He tells you to go next door and witness to your neighbor, you need to obey the Lord. Even after honoring the Lord's instructions, you are still not earning anything from Him. You are simply operating in faith. On the other hand, if you witness to your neighbor every day, because you think you can merit something from God, or you think He will owe you something for your efforts, then you're operating in works of the flesh, and not works of faith. The Lord doesn't owe me healing because I read a certain amount of chapters in the Bible or pray a certain length of time each day. He's provided healing for me, freely from His grace, but I must receive it by faith.

Luke 5:18-20 says:
"Then behold, men brought on a bed a man who was paralyzed, whom they sought to bring in and lay before Him.
And when they could not find how they might bring him in, because of the crowd, they went up on the housetop and let him down with his bed through the tiling into the midst before Jesus.
<u>When He saw their faith</u>, He said to him, "Man, your sins are forgiven you.""

The Bible says that Jesus saw their faith. You can't

see faith with your natural eyes, but you can see <u>works</u> of faith. The man on the cot and the men carrying him were acting in faith when they came to Jesus. They wouldn't have brought him if they didn't believe he would be healed. Now, they didn't earn healing for the man, because that's a benefit of grace. It's free. But notice, they still had to operate in faith to appropriate it for the man. In verse 17, the Bible says that power of the Lord was present to heal everyone. So, healing was free for everyone there, but only one man received it, according to the Biblical record, and he happened to be the only one who operated in faith. Faith and grace always work together. You don't have one without the other.

Let's look at something else about salvation in Romans 10:9,

"That if you confess with your mouth the Lord Jesus and believe in your heart that God has raised Him from the dead, you <u>will be saved</u>.

God said you <u>will be </u>saved. He didn't say you're already saved. He said the way to be saved is to confess Jesus as your Lord and believe in your heart that God raised Him from the dead. If you haven't done that, you're not saved. Again, it doesn't matter what your denomination says or what the minister says. You better obey God and not man. Remember,

True Salvation

Romans 3:4 says to let God be true and every man a liar! Look at verse 13:

"For "whoever calls on the name of the Lord shall be saved.""

He said <u>shall be</u> saved. He didn't say the person is already saved. Now that Jesus has died and arose from the dead, every person still must call on His Name to be saved, or to experience what He obtained for him. Also, think about what the Apostle Paul said concerning Israel in Romans 11:25-27. He's writing about the nation of Israel after Calvary had taken place. He's referring to the future, something that hasn't happened yet. He said all of Israel <u>will be</u> saved, meaning all of them are not saved yet. That tells me they will have to appropriate their salvation by faith to receive the grace of salvation. In Revelation 22:17, the Spirit of God said, **"...Whoever desires, let him <u>take the water</u> of life freely."** If everybody is already saved, then why would they need to take the water of life freely? Once again, Jesus died for us and arose from the dead, so that salvation would be a (free) gift to us. But like any gift, you still must reach out and take it, or you will never enjoy your free gift. God's blessings don't fall on us like ripe apples off a tree. <u>We must</u> receive them through our faith in God!

True Repentance

3

First Love

In Revelation, chapters 2 & 3, the Lord Jesus dictated letters to seven different churches. He gave them to the Apostle John to make the delivery. In all seven letters, one phrase is repeated every time. The phrase is, <u>I know your works</u>. It's very true that God sees and knows our hearts, but He didn't say to each church, "I see your hearts". Here is something you may have heard many times after encouraging a fellow Believer to read his Bible, pray and go to church. The excuse the fellow Christian will use is, "God knows my heart. Even though I don't go to church or serve the Lord like I should; He still knows my heart, and He knows I love Him." Apparently, those particular Christians have not read I John 2:3,4.

"Now by this we know that we know Him, if we keep His commandments.
He who says, "I know Him," and does not keep

His commandments, is a liar, and the truth is not in him."

Yes, God does know our hearts, but that is not what Jesus said to the seven churches. He said, "I see your works." Obviously, works are very important to the Lord, not works of the flesh (meaning works we are doing to earn something from God), but works of faith (works that are the result of obedience to God). For example, because I love Jesus, I want to preach His Word and tell others about Him. Those are works of faith. I'm not doing them to merit something from Him. I'm doing them because I want to, whether I get any rewards or not. I obey God because I want to, but since He's so good, He will always bless me back, but I'm not earning that blessing; it's coming freely from His grace.

Let's look at Revelation 2:1-5,

"To the angel of the church of Ephesus write, These things says He who holds the seven stars in His right hand, who walks in the midst of the seven golden lamp stands:

I know your works, your labor, your patience, and that you cannot bear those who are evil. And you have tested those who say they are apostles and are not, and have found them liars;

And you have persevered and have patience,

First Love

and have labored for My name's sake and have not become weary.

Nevertheless I have this against you, that <u>you have left your first love</u>.

Remember therefore from where you have fallen; repent and do the first works, or else I will come to you quickly and remove your lamp stand from its place-unless you repent."

If you notice in this letter to the church at Ephesus, the Lord first praised them for their great works, but then, to their surprise and our surprise, He rebuked them. He didn't rebuke them for their sinning, or breaking His commandments. He told them what a great job they had been doing in their service to Him, but then told them they left their first love. You know they were probably feeling a little confused. They were probably thinking, "We have been doing all these good works because of our love for You." What happened here? How could they do so many wonderful things for God and His Kingdom, and then quit honoring Him as their first love?

I believe this was a very clever deception from the devil that they fell into. It was so subtle they didn't realize it was happening, until it was too late. There's a lesson here we definitely need to learn. The key is in verse five. Jesus said to repent and do the <u>first works.</u> Why the first works? Even though their latter works had been Biblical and Godly, their first works were tied in to their "first love", the latter were not. Their first works were a result of falling in love with Jesus. They were works produced from a close relationship with the Lord. But somewhere down the line they allowed their good works to come between them and their relationship with Jesus. They got so busy working for the Lord, they quit spending time with Him, and He actually lost first place in their lives.

Here's how the devil works. If he can't stop you from serving the Lord, then he will try a reverse strategy on you. He will try to get you so busy serving the Lord (and you won't think twice about it because you know you're blessing the Kingdom and helping people), you will spend less and less time in real fellowship with Him. My wife and I travel and teach supernatural evangelism meetings, where we train Believers in how to operate in their ministries, but our passion for Christ has to be greater than our passion for souls. As much as we love training Believers and making disciples, we love Jesus the most! The only thing more exciting than winning the lost to Jesus is knowing Him! <u>Don't ever substitute passion for souls, for passion for Christ</u>! Let me give you a very important statement that Oswald Chambers wrote years ago.

First Love

"You have to learn to go out of convictions, out of creeds, out of experiences, until so far as your faith is concerned there is nothing between yourself and God."

My relationship is between me and God, not me and my works. Good works should always be the outcome of a close walk with the Lord. Good works are very important, but don't ever allow anything to come between you and God, no matter how good it may be, for that's idolatry. I Corinthians 15:58 says:

"Therefore, my beloved brethren, be steadfast, immovable, always abounding in the work of the Lord, knowing that your labor is not in vain in the Lord."

To abound in the work of the Lord, is not to the exclusion of spending personal time with Him. What we must practice every day (and you decide how long), is to fellowship with the Lord. Spend time in prayer (your known language and tongues), meditate God's Word and listen to His voice. Take time in your fellowship with the Lord just to be quiet and listen to His voice, because He wants to talk to us. Expect to hear God's voice! This is how we stay strong and at rest in Him, no matter how busy we are. Also, it's how we avoid "burn out". We will never experience

True Repentance

"burn out" if we follow the witness of the Holy Spirit within us. Burn out comes when we get over in the flesh, wanting to implement our ideas, instead of trusting God. If we keep the Lord Jesus as our first love, we will always live a life of peace and victory. We will be a great example to others of what it means to be steadfast, immovable and always abounding in the work of the Lord!

About the Author

Dwayne Norman is a 1978 graduate of Christ For The Nations Bible Institute in Dallas, Texas. He spent 3 years witnessing to prostitutes and pimps in the red light district of Dallas, and another 3 years ministering as a team leader in the Campus Challenge ministry of Dr. Norvel Hayes. He was ordained by Pastor Buddy and Pat Harrison of Faith Christian Fellowship in Tulsa, Oklahoma in September 1980, and is part of Dr. Ed Dufresne's Fresh Oil Fellowship. He also taught evangelism classes several times at Dr. Hayes' Bible school in Tennessee.

Soon the Lord led him to go on the road ministering. He ministers powerfully on soul winning, and on how God wants to use all Believers in demonstrating His Kingdom not just in Word but also in Power!

He teaches with clarity, the work that God accomplished for all believers in Christ from the cross to the throne, and the importance of this revelation to the church for the fulfillment of Jesus' commission to make disciples of all nations.

He strongly believes that we are called to do the works Jesus did and greater works in His Name, not just in church but especially in the market place. As a result Dwayne experiences many healing miracles in his services, arms and legs growing out, as well as other miracles.

He and his wife Leia travel and teach Supernatural Evangelism and train Believers in who they are in Christ and how to operate in their ministries.

To inquire for meetings with Dwayne & Leia Norman, please contact them at:

Dwayne & Leia Norman
124 Evergreen Court
Mt. Sterling, KY 40353

(859) 351-6496
dwayne7@att.net
Web: www.dwaynenormanministries.org

Contact Dwayne to order his other books and products:

The Mystery DVD's (12 hours)	$50.00
The Mystery (book)	$12.00
The Mystery Study Guide	$10.00
The Awesome Power in the Message of the Cross	$10.00
Your Beginning with God	$10.00
The Law of the Spirit Of Life in Christ Jesus	$10.00
Demonstrating God's Kingdom	$10.00

www.ingramcontent.com/pod-product-compliance
Lightning Source LLC
Chambersburg PA
CBHW061348040426
42444CB00011B/3138